THE ULTIMATE GUIDE TO BASKETBALL

Published in the UK by Scholastic Children's Books, 2020
Euston House, 24 Eversholt Street, London, NW1 1DB
A division of Scholastic Limited

London ~ New York ~ Toronto ~ Sydney ~ Auckland
Mexico City ~ New Delhi ~ Hong Kong

SCHOLASTIC and associated logos are trademarks and/or
registered trademarks of Scholastic Inc.

Text by Emily Stead © Scholastic Children's Books
Cover photography © Getty Images

ISBN 978 07023 0575 7

A CIP catalogue record for this book is available from the British Library.

Printed and bound in the UK by Bell and Bain Ltd, Glasgow
Papers used by Scholastic Children's Books are made from wood grown in
sustainable forests.

2 4 6 8 10 9 7 5 3 1

www.scholastic.co.uk

THE ULTIMATE GUIDE TO BASKETBALL

SCHOLASTIC

CONTENTS

MY BASKETBALL PROFILE

Welcome, basketball fan! If you were born to shoot hoops and make slam dunks in your sleep, then this book is your ultimate guide to conquering the court! Fill in your player profile on the next page.

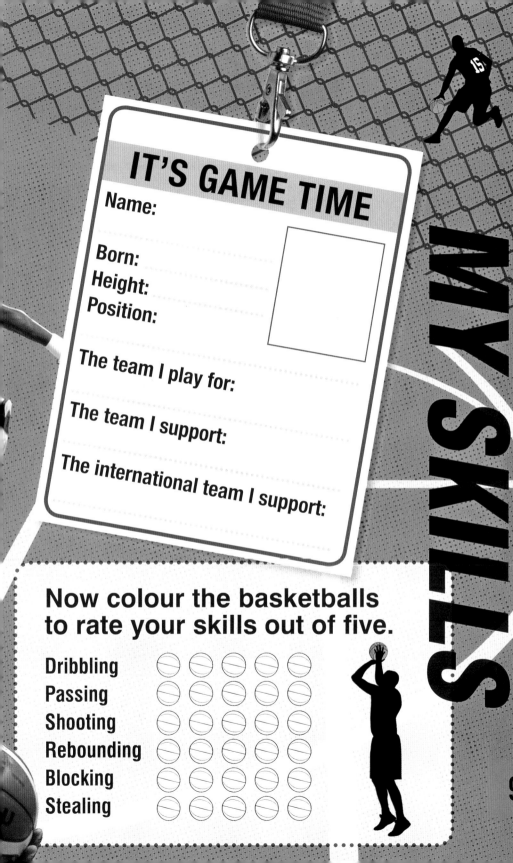

IT'S GAME TIME

Name:

Born:

Height:

Position:

The team I play for:

The team I support:

The international team I support:

Now colour the basketballs
to rate your skills out of five.

Dribbling ⊖ ⊖ ⊖ ⊖ ⊖

Passing ⊖ ⊖ ⊖ ⊖ ⊖

Shooting ⊖ ⊖ ⊖ ⊖ ⊖

Rebounding ⊖ ⊖ ⊖ ⊖ ⊖

Blocking ⊖ ⊖ ⊖ ⊖ ⊖

Stealing ⊖ ⊖ ⊖ ⊖ ⊖

Basketball was invented by Canadian-born James Naismith in 1891. At the time, Naismith was working as a PE teacher at Springfield YMCA International Training School in Massachusetts, USA. He designed the indoor game to encourage his students to keep up their fitness levels over winter, when they couldn't play American Football.

The game was designed to be played by two teams, with the object to score more points than the other team by throwing a football into a basket. Initially, the goals were made from two **peach baskets** and attached to the rail of Springfield's

gymnasium balcony, which was just over 3 m (10 ft) from the ground. As the game developed, the baskets were placed at the top of long metal poles. Finally, holes were made in the bottom of the baskets, so that the ball could be retrieved more easily.

Naismith wrote 13 rules for his game dubbed **'basketball'** and published them in the college's newspaper, *The Triangle*, in January 1892. The rules have been tweaked over the years but remain largely as Naismith originally stated. In 1894, an official ball produced by Spalding was introduced, although it wasn't until 1906 that metal hoops, nets and backboards were used.

GROWING THE GAME

The YMCA (Young Men's Christian Association) and the US Army both played an important part in helping the sport to spread throughout North America and beyond. In 1893, Melvin Rideout, one of Naismith's original players, introduced the game at the YMCA's new outpost in Paris, France. Rideout oversaw the first basketball game played on

European soil and, to this day, the Paris indoor court remains on of the oldest basketball courts in the world.

The game then spread further across Europe, to Belgium, Spain, Portugal and Russia – all countries where basketball remains a top sport today. It was introduced in Brazil in 1894, where the game first took off among women, while men played football, which was exported to the country around the same time. By the time US troops joined the British First World War effort in Europe in 1917, thousands of men and women were familiar with basketball.

COLLEGE BASKETBALL

Matches between American colleges have been played since 1895. The first college game featuring five players per side was between Iowa and Chicago in 1896. At the turn of the century, basketball had spread to colleges throughout the United States. Basketball continues to dominate college sport today.

International First

The first international match took place in 1909 in Saint Petersburg, as a Russian side beat an American YMCA team. Ten years later, a tournament between the United States, Italy and France held in Paris helped to further boost the sport's appeal in Europe. FIBA, the International Basketball Federation, was later founded in 1932, to organize competitions globally. Their work saw men's basketball included at the 1936 Berlin Olympic Games for the first time.

Going Pro

A professional basketball league was formed in New York in 1946 as the BAA (Basketball Association of America). It would later become the NBA (National Basketball Association). Since its launch, the league has attracted the biggest global stars and produced some of the most exciting matches in basketball history. You can read more about the **NBA** on pages 38–39.

Basketball Today

NBA heroes such as Michael Jordan and Yao Ming have helped basketball reach international audiences and grow into one of the most popular sports in the world. Today, FIBA estimates that at least 450 million people play basketball globally, while millions more fans enjoy watching elite matches streamed live from around the world. So, whether you want to get involved as a fan or a player, there's a team out there for everyone.

15

Major Milestones in the Game

1891 **James Naismith** invents a game where players score by throwing the ball into peach baskets.

1892 In January, Naismith names his game **'basketball'** and publishes a list of 13 rules. The first public basketball game is played in Springfield, Massachusetts, on 11 March.

1896 The first professional basketball game is played in Trenton, New Jersey, USA. Trenton YMCA defeat Brooklyn YMCA 15–1.

1906 **Peach baskets** for scoring are finally replaced by metal hoops with backboards.

1932 The International Basketball Association **(FIBA)**, an organization to govern the sport globally is established.

1946 The Basketball Association of America **(BAA)** is founded in New York City on 6 June.

1937 The National Basketball League **(NBL)** is formed with 13 teams competing in the league that year.

1940 The first game to be **televised** takes place at Madison Square Gardens, New York. The University of Pittsburgh beat Fordham 57–37.

1946 The Basketball Association of America **(BAA)** is founded in New York City on 6 June.

1945 **Wheelchair basketball** is first played at two USA World War II veterans' administration hospitals in Corona Naval Station, California and Framingham, Massachusetts.

1949 The 11-team BAA merges with the National Basketball League, which has six teams. Together, they form the National Basketball Association **(NBA)**.

1956 Basketball for wheelchair athletes features at the 1956 International Stoke Mandeville Games for the first time. The competition is the forerunner of the Paralympic Games.

1961 **Wilt Chamberlain** sets the NBA scoring record on 2 March by tallying 100 points for the Philadelphia Warriors in a 169–147 victory over the New York Knicks.

1979 **Chris Ford** of the Boston Celtics makes the first three-point shot on 12 October against the Houston Rockets.

1983 The Detroit Pistons defeat the Denver Nuggets 186–184 in the **highest-scoring** game in NBA history.

1989 FIBA allows professional NBA players to compete at future Olympic Games.

1992 The USA's **'Dream Team'** win gold at the 1992 Olympic Games in Barcelona.

1996 The NBA establishes the Women's National Basketball Association **(WNBA)**, with play beginning the following year.

2020 Play in both the NBA and WNBA is suspended mid-season due to the coronavirus pandemic.

BASKETBALL BASICS

Basketball is an exciting sport to watch and play, with a simple set of rules. Once you know the basics, you can enjoy this fast-paced game all year round. Two teams score points by shooting a ball into the opposing team's basket and the team that scores the most points wins.

Five players make up each team, with substitute players on the bench.

The game is played on a rectangular floor called a court, with a hoop at each end.

When played indoors, the playing surface is made from polished hardwood. Most players first learn the sport on outdoor courts.

The mid-court line divides the court into two equal halves. In professional basketball, once the attacking team puts the ball into play behind this line, it has eight seconds to get the ball over the mid-court line, by dribbling or passing. If it doesn't, play is awarded to the defensive team.

The ball is moved down the court towards the basket by passing or dribbling. The defensive team must try to steal the ball, intercept shots and passes and collect rebounds.

The rules on this page follow FIBA's official basketball guidelines.

three-point arc

lane, key, or paint

free throw line

top of the key/circle

baseline

wing

midcourt line

sideline

corner

SCORING

When a team makes a basket, they score two points and the ball goes to the other team. If a basket, or field goal, is made from outside the three-point arc, it is worth three points. A free throw, awarded for a foul, is worth one point. If a player is fouled beyond the three-point line, they are awarded three free throws. Within the arc, two free shots are given for a foul.

THE CLOCK

A professional game of basketball is made up of four quarters, each lasting 12 minutes, while games for younger players are shorter. Teams swap ends each quarter. The clock is stopped whenever the ball goes out of play. If the game is tied after the fourth quarter, it continues with an extra period of five minutes, then further five-minute periods until one team outscores the other.

FOULS AND VIOLATIONS

Any physical contact such as holding, pushing, slapping or blocking is illegal. The umpire awards a foul and play is given to the opposing team. Other violations include walking or travelling – where a player takes more than one or two steps without dribbling the ball. Carrying or palming the ball is also against the rules of play, as is a 'double dribble' – dribbling the ball with both hands on the ball at the same time.

The five players in a basketball team generally take up specific positions: *point guard*, *shooting guard*, *small forward*, *power forward* and *centre*. Take a look at the skills and qualities required to shine in each position.

POINT GUARD

The **point guard** (PG) is the playmaker, serving a key role in the team's performance on the court. They must have excellent passing and ball-handling skills to set up other players to score – PGs often make the most assists. Their shooting must be strong too, to score three-pointers themselves. They are often the shortest players on the team.

Skills: speed, creative passing, ball-handling, shooting from distance
Famous Point Guards: Magic Johnson, Stephen Curry, Diana Taurasi

SHOOTING GUARD

As the name suggests, the **shooting guard's** main job is to put the ball in the hoop, whether it's from outside, mid-range or close to the basket. They should be strong dribblers and need to be able to find space on the court to score when not in possession of the ball.

Skills: shooting, ball-handling, strong defence
Famous Shooting Guards: Michael Jordan, Kobe Bryant and James Harden

SMALL FORWARD

Don't let the name fool you – the **small forward** has a big role to play for the team. Playing this position requires a mix of skills including strong ball-handling, rebounding and the ability to shoot from outside and inside positions. Small forwards work hard for the team, drawing fouls and driving towards the basket.

Skills: versatility, speed, guarding multiple positions
Famous Small Forwards: LeBron James, Tamika Catchings and Ovie Soko

POWER FORWARD

The team's **power forward** is often the second-tallest player and must possess skill and strength, outmuscling opponents off the ball. Power forwards play close to the basket when shooting, but they also need a good jump shot to score maximum points.

Skills: height, strength, range of shots, rebounding
Famous Power Forwards: Tim Duncan, Dennis Rodman and Candace Parker

CENTRE

Usually the tallest and most athletic person on the team, a **centre** defends the basket at one end of the court while proving a menace at the other. Professional male centres usually measure 2 m 08 cm (6 ft 9 in) tall or above. They often score most of their points by staying close to the basket and scoring from rebounds.

Skills: height, strength, shot-blocking, rebounding
Famous Centres: Shaquille O'Neal, Joel Embiid and Kareem Abdul-Jabbar

BENCH

The first player to come off the **bench** is known as the **'6th man'**. They are valuable players who are often as skilled as the starting five and can make a big impact on the game. Usually two to four more players sit on the sideline and make up the rest of the 'bench'.

WHAT POSITION SHOULD I PLAY?

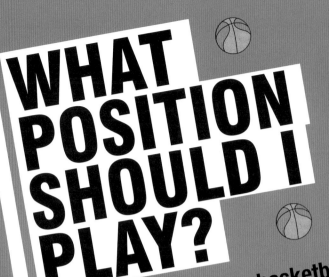

So, you want to play basketball but aren't sure where you line up? Choosing the right position should play to the strengths and weaknesses of your game. Take this quiz to discover your best position on the court.

1. How do you measure up?

A. I'm shorter (but louder) than my teammates!

B. I'm not the tallest but I'm a sure shot.

C. I'm pretty tall with great reach.

D. I tower well above my friends and classmates.

E. If they gave medals for growing, I'd win gold!

2. How fast are your feet?

A. Lightning speed is one of my best qualities.

B. I get up and down the wing in record time.

C. Fit and fast, I make others look slow.

D. My game combines speed with style.

E. Being light on my feet is not my strong suit.

3. How sharp is your shooting?

A. My skills lie in creating chances for others.

B. I'll take a shot whenever I get the chance.

C. Scoring in the paint is what I do best.

D. The team depends on me to rack up the points.

E. Not always perfect, but I'm top at rebounds.

4. How chatty are you on court?

A. I'm a natural leader, not afraid to give my team instructions.

B. I'm pretty laid back and let others take the lead.

C. I prefer to let my dribbling do the talking.

D. I do less talking, more dunking!

E. I use my voice to put off my opponents.

5. Which of the following excites you?

A. Coaching my team to victory.

B. Throwing a killer pass.

C. Performing a powerful slam dunk.

D. Scoring a special three-pointer.

E. Making the perfect block.

6. Which other sport do you most enjoy playing?

A. Ice hockey.

B. Football.

C. Long-distance running.

D. American football or rugby.

E. Weightlifting.

7. Who is your ultimate basketball hero?

A. Stephen Curry.

B. Michael Jordan.

C. LeBron James.

D. Tim Duncan.

E. Shaquille O'Neal.

Now add up your answers to see how you scored.

Mostly As
POINT GUARD

If you talk a good game and can influence others, you'd make a perfect point guard. You'll need great mobility and fast feet too, as you'll cover most of the court during a game.

Mostly Bs
SHOOTING GUARD

Your no.1 skill is shooting – from anywhere on the court. You should be comfortable playing under pressure and be ever-ready to take on taller and tougher opponents.

Mostly Cs
SMALL FORWARD

Tall and athletic, small forward could suit you. You'll need amazing ball-handling skills, great vision and the ability to create scoring opportunities for teammates to succeed.

Mostly Ds
POWER FORWARD

As one of the tallest in the team, protecting the paint and providing solid rebounds are top priorities for a power forward. If you have both the height and strength, give this position a go.

Mostly Es
CENTRE

Super-tall and super-strong, you're great at blocking shots and busting in rebounds. You love to defend and play with your back to the basket – centre could be your best position.

DRIBBLING

Dribbling is an important skill that every basketball player should master. Get to grips with the basics and learn how to move the ball across the court. With plenty of practice, you'll soon be dribbling like a pro.

1. Use your fingertips rather than the palm of your hand to control the ball and spread out your fingers.

2. Position your body low to the ground, with your feet shoulder-width apart. Bend your knees and keep your chest upright.

3. Use your dominant hand to bounce the ball firmly on the ground. Push the ball down using your fingertips each time and keep your hand on top of the ball.

4. Keep the bounces short, quick and low to the ground, making it harder for your opponent to steal the ball.

5. Practise moving around the court with your head up, so you are aware of where your teammates and opponents are positioned.

6. Position your body between the defender and the ball to make it difficult for the defender to steal the ball from you.

7. Look to pass to a teammate if they are in a better position to shoot.

TOP TIP

As you become more confident, try using both hands to dribble the ball.

27

PASSING

Passing a basketball between teammates is a key skill that all players should practise regularly, as every effective offensive move requires it.

Chest Pass

Passing is a faster way to move the ball up the court than dribbling. The chest pass is a basic pass that is direct, accurate and easy to receive. Here's how to make one...

1. Stand with your feet shoulder-width apart and your knees bent.

2. Hold the ball close to your chest with both hands, with your fingers spread around it.

3. Step forwards as you release the ball, extending your arms towards your teammate.

4. Finish the pass with your thumbs together pointing downwards and your fingers facing your target.

TOP TIP

Use your eyes to fool defenders into thinking you are about to make a pass in a different direction.

Bounce Pass

A bounce pass is a quick, short pass that can be used to find a teammate in a crowd of players. This low pass is difficult for opponents to steal.

1. Stand with your feet shoulder-width apart and your knees bent.

2. Place both hands on either side of the ball, with your fingers spread apart.

3. With the ball at waist level, step forwards, aiming your pass at the floor in the direction of your teammate.

4. Flick your wrists with your thumbs pointing towards the floor to release the ball.

5. Finish with arms in front of you at thigh height.

TOP TIP

Aim to bounce the ball three-quarters of the way between you and your teammate, so the pass bounces up for your teammate to catch at chest level.

SHOOTING

The game of basketball is all about scoring points, with shooting an all-important skill. From the slam dunk to the three-point shot from distance, there are a range of shots to learn. With enough practice, you can master them all.

Lay-up

A lay-up is a basic shot where the backboard is used to bounce the ball into the net. When attempting a lay-up, approach the basket from the left or right side. Make your jump towards the basket, aiming to bounce the ball in off the backboard.

TOP TIP

A good player should have a range of shots that they can call upon in different game situations. Work on close-range and distance shots equally.

Dunk

A dunk or slam dunk is where the attacker leaps above the rim and slams the ball through the net. As the hoop is usually around 3 m (10 ft) from the ground, not many players have the height to pull off this shot. It does look spectacular when performed, though!

Jump Shot

Just as it sounds, the jump shot is where a player jumps into the air before releasing the shot. This shot can be used to gain height and can be taken from anywhere on the court. Plant your feet, then release the ball at the highest point of your jump. Keep practising, as it can take a while to master.

Hook Shot

A hook shot is tough to stop. Typically made with one hand, it creates extra height when close to the basket. When in position, release the ball using one hand, using your other hand to defend yourself. Push your shooting arm up and over your head, then flick your wrist as you release the ball from your fingertips. Follow through towards the basket with your shooting arm.

Free Throw

A free throw is awarded following a foul. When taking the throw, a player's feet must remain behind the free throw line until the ball is released. The shot relies on good upper body strength.

REBOUNDING

Rebounding is when a player gains possession of a basketball following a missed shot. After the ball has bounced off the rim or backboard, try to grab the ball quickly to get a rebound, whoever has taken the shot. Both defensive and offensive players should look for rebounds.

TOP TIP

Most first shots in basketball are missed – even at pro level. Pay attention to where shots are made from and move to the part of the court where they are likely to rebound.

1. Before the shot is even taken, find a good position on the court.

2. If none of your teammates are close to the hoop, move in to get the rebound.

3. If you made the shot yourself, follow it in to the basket to try to win your own rebound.

4. Spread your arms out wide to block other players and be ready to catch the ball.

5. As soon as the ball hits the rim or backboard, move quickly to meet it.

6. Always try to grab the ball with both hands when you jump, then hug it towards your body.

7. As you land, raise the ball up to your chin, ready to shoot again or pass to a teammate.

BLOCKING

The defensive art of blocking shots is key to stopping your opponents from scoring. This important skill is often the difference between winning and losing games, but players need to learn to block without giving away a foul.

1. When attempting to block a shot, remember to jump upwards, using your body as a barrier between your opponent and the hoop. This will reduce the chance of you making contact with the player, resulting in a foul.

2. A defender's height and size are crucial, though agility is essential to helping you get into a position to be able to make the block. Add some running and rotating drills to your training sessions.

3. Keep your feet evenly spaced apart, and parallel, rather than one foot in front of the other. As you prepare for the block, squat down to give you lift.

4. Work on the timing of your jump – you want to jump up to meet your opponent at their highest point. Watch when their feet leave the ground and make your move.

5. Use the hand that is closest to block the arc of the ball. Get used to blocking with both hands, rather than your favoured one.

6. Effective blocking comes with practice, practice and more practice, so train with other players whenever you get the opportunity.

TOP TIP

To be a top shot blocker work on your vertical jumps to increase your reach in the air.

STEALING

A steal in basketball is where one team takes possession of the ball from the other. A player can either use their hand to swipe the ball out of the dribbler's hands or intercept a pass. Again, making physical contact with an opponent is forbidden, resulting in a free throw for the opposition.

1. Look out for players who are weaker dribblers or who leave the ball exposed when they pick it up.

2. Don't give the dribbler a lot of room – get low, bending your knees to stay close.

3. Try to anticipate where the dribbler is going and force them out towards the boundary lines. Be ready to swipe when they make a mistake.

4. Jab at the ball a few times to keep the dribbler guessing when you're about to steal.

5. Show your determination to win the ball without being too aggressive – you don't want to foul.

TOP TIP

If you're positioned in between two opponents, try to keep your eyes on both the passer and the receiver.

PRO LEAGUES
NBA

From the league's beginnings in the 1940s, the National Basketball Association (NBA) and its stars have blazed a trail for elite basketball around the world. Many believe the Chicago Bulls during the 1990s to be the greatest NBA side ever, when Michael Jordan lit up the court, while the Boston Celtics dominated in previous decades. The LA Lakers have been the strongest team this century. For top stars and thrilling action, no league in the world can match the NBA.

The **Golden State Warriors** won the championship in 2015, 2017 and 2018, making them one of the NBA's top teams.

PROFILE

Founded: 1946

Number of teams: 30

Most titles: Boston Celtics (17)

Notable teams: Boston Celtics, Chicago Bulls, LA Lakers

Greek Hero

From sharing trainers with his brother in Athens to being named **NBA MVP** for 2018–19, **Giannis Antetokounmpo's** basketball journey has been nothing short of incredible. The Milwaukee Bucks' forward is known for his sky-hooking dunks and pace in the paint. Still in his mid-20s, this all-star is set for more sensational seasons.

King Kareem

Kareem Abdul-Jabbar played as a centre for the Milwaukee Bucks and the LA Lakers over three decades until his retirement in 1989, aged 42. He was the **NBA MVP** six times and still leads the all-time scoring records in the league's history, with an untouchable 38,387 points scored in just over the 1,500 games he played. Unsurprisingly, Abdul-Jabbar is considered to be basketball's greatest ever centre.

CBA

The Chinese Basketball Association (CBA) is the top league in Asia. Its first season was 1995–96, and its popularity has grown each year. The Bayi Rockets won the opening six championships, while the current league winners are the Guangdong Southern Tigers. Only a limited number of foreign players are allowed on each CBA team, with imports from the NBA and Europe having helped to raise standards of play and draw new fans over the years.

PROFILE

Founded: 1995
Number of teams: 20
Most titles: Guangdong Southern Tigers (9)
Notable teams: Bayi Rockets, Guangdong Southern Tigers, Beijing Ducks

Excellent Export

Yao Ming is one of China's best-known athletes and is the CBA's most famous export to the NBA. He began his career with the Shanghai Sharks, but was drafted by the **Houston Rockets** in 2002. The centre star, measuring 2 m 29 cm (7 ft 6 in) tall, attracted huge crowds wherever Houston played, and the Rockets' games were broadcast throughout Asia.

Lin-credible

After signing with the Golden State Warriors in 2010, **Jeremy Lin** became the first American of Chinese or Taiwanese descent to play in the NBA. Lin soon became an inspiring figure for many Asian Americans. During his 2011–12 season with the New York Knicks, "Linsanity" swept across his fans as Lin's popularity soared. In 2019, Lin became the first Asian American to win an NBA championship with the Toronto Raptors. As well as American basketball, Lin signed with the Beijing Ducks of the CBA in 2019.

PRO LEAGUES

BBL

BRITISH BASKETBALL LEAGUE

The British Basketball League (BBL) is made up of 11 teams from England and Scotland. The league has been running for over 30 years and has experienced seesawing fortunes as basketball's popularity has grown in the UK. Squads are mostly made up of British players, although clubs can register players from other countries. Fans can expect top talent on show and end-to-end action.

42

PROFILE

Newcastle Eagles have been crowned BBL champions more times than any other team.

Founded: 1996
Number of teams: 11
Most titles: Newcastle Eagles (7)
Notable teams: Newcastle Eagles, Leicester Riders, London Lions

Leading Lion

British point guard Justin Robinson has been named the league's MVP for the past two seasons (2017–18 and 2018–19), representing London Lions. London-born Robinson spent his high school and college years in the United States, though returned to Europe to begin his pro basketball career with Greek club side, Maroussi.

Record Breaker

Peter Scantlebury leads the league's all-time scoring charts with 9,502 points, earned with seven different clubs. He was a BBL champion nine times and only missed one match in 23 years! When his playing days were over, he became England's national coach.

PRO LEAGUES
BASKETBALL IN EUROPE

Basketball has been played in Europe almost as long as in the United States, with the earliest game recorded in Paris, France, in 1893. Some of the oldest professional basketball leagues are based on the continent, and the EuroLeague is the sport's second-largest competition after the NBA. European basketball is known for its stylish passing play and shot accuracy.

EuroLeague

The EuroLeague is similar to football's UEFA Champions League, with the top European clubs qualifying each year. The competition was rebranded in 2000 by FIBA and games are played midweek. **CSKA Moscow** are the current champions while Real Madrid have won the most titles **(ten)**.

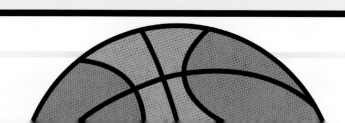

Liga ACB

The ACB is Spain's top basketball league. Formed in 1983, the competition has been dominated by two teams attached to Spain's premier football clubs – FC Barcelona and Real Madrid, who have shared 28 of all 37 titles between them. Matches attract crowds of over 6,000 fans, who flock to see home-grown stars such as Real's **Sergio Llull**.

LNB Pro A

France's Pro A league, known as the Jeep Élite, has a rich history and was formed back in 1920. ASVEL, based in Lyon, have won the most league titles with 19, while Limoges CSP have 11. Limoges are also the only French team to have been a European champion, winning the EuroLeague in the 1990s.

OTHER NOTABLE LEAGUES

- Basketball Bundesliga **(BBL)**
- Basketball Super League **(BSL)**
- VTB United League
- Lega Basket Serie A **(LBA)**

WOMEN'S BASKETBALL

Women's basketball was developed in the late nineteenth century alongside the men's game in the United States. Its popularity steadily grew throughout North America and Europe over the next decades and the FIBA Women's Basketball World Cup was first held in 1953. The sport did not feature at an Olympic Games until 1976, although it has been included ever since. The United States women's team have won an incredible eight gold medals.

CHANGING THE GAME

Women play with a slightly smaller ball, measuring 2 m 54 cm (1 inch) smaller than a men's regulation basketball, while the three-point line is also 91 cm (3 ft) closer to the basket than on an average NBA court.

Mother of Basketball

Senda Berenson was the trailblazing director of physical education at Smith College in Northampton, Massachusetts, in the late nineteenth century. She adapted Naismith's rules of the game to suit her female classes and **wrote the first basketball guide for women**.

Golden Girl

USA forward **Tamika Catchings** is one of the game's most decorated players. Now retired, she began her international career while still in high school and went on to win four Olympic gold medals and two FIBA World Championships. The free-scoring forward was a WNBA champion in 2012 with Indiana Fever, when she was named **MVP** for the season.

WHEELCHAIR BASKETBALL

Wheelchair basketball is as fast and furious as regulation basketball. Played on a standard-size court, each team has 12 players, with five on court at any one time. The game is split into four periods of ten minutes and fouls are awarded when wheelchairs come into contact with each other.

Following the Second World War, wheelchair basketball games were played between disabled American veterans. An international competition later featured at the 1956 International Stoke Mandeville Games, while wheelchair netball had been played at earlier editions.

TOP COMPETITIONS

Wheelchair basketball has featured in every **Paralympic Games** since these were introduced in 1960. The Wheelchair Basketball World Championship was first held in Belgium in 1973. The two competitions now alternate every two years.

Matt Scott is a four-time Paralympian who won gold for the United States at the 2016 Rio Paralympic Games.

GIANNIS ANTETOKOUNMPO

THE MILWAUKEE BUCKS' STAR PLAYMAKER

PROFILE

Position: power forward
National team: Greece
Current team: Milwaukee Bucks
Born: 6 December, 1994
Height: 2 m 11 cm
(6 ft 11 in)

Born in Greece to Nigerian parents, Antetokounmpo discovered a talent for basketball as a teenager growing up in Athens. Tall and athletic, he was scouted by Filathlitikos in the Greek league as a teenager. In 2013, at the age of 18, he was drafted by the NBA team Milwaukee Bucks on a rookie contract, and has since played for the side in all five positions. His vision, assists and ball-handling skills have seen Antetokounmpo develop into one of the top all-round players in the NBA, earning him the MVP in 2019.

PROFILE

Position: point guard
National team: USA
Current team: Golden State Warriors
Born: 14 March, 1988
Height: 1 m 91 cm (6 ft 3 in)

Rakuten

GOLDEN STATE
30
WARRIORS

STEPHEN CURRY
STEPH 'CHEF CURRY' HAS SUPERB SHOOTING SKILLS

Curry has won multiple NBA championships and twice been named MVP with the Golden State Warriors, which is said to be one of the best teams in NBA history. Playing as a point guard, Curry has helped to change the game by inspiring teams to score more three-pointers. Despite not being among the tallest or most physical players, Curry has one of the best shots in the world. Both his dad and brother have been NBA stars too!

51

ANTHONY DAVIS
THE MASTER OF THE INSIDE-OUT DRIBBLE!

PROFILE
· · · · · · · · · · · · · · · · · · ·

Position: power forward, centre
National team: USA
Current team: LA Lakers
Born: 11 March, 1993
Height: 2 m 08 cm
(6 ft 10 in)

Playing number 3 for the Los Angeles Lakers, Davis is a top shot blocker, who can dribble with speed and score three-pointers too. A growth spurt at high school saw him become one of the hottest recruits in the NBA and he began his pro career with the New Orleans Pelicans (then Hornets), aged 19. The seven-time All-Star has twice won gold with the USA, at the London 2012 London Olympic Games and the 2014 FIBA World Cup.

PROFILE
· · · · · · · · · · · · · · · · · · · ·

Position: small forward,
power forward
National team: USA
Current team: Brooklyn Nets
Born: 29 September, 1988
Height: 2 m 08 cm
(6 ft 10 in)

KEVIN DURANT

A FORWARD WHO ENJOYED A RAPID RISE TO THE TOP

Measuring over six foot in high school, Durant was destined to be an NBA great. After just one season playing college basketball, the forward was drafted by the Seattle SuperSonics and earned Rookie of the Year in his first pro season. His first NBA championships came back-to-back in 2017 and 2018 with the Golden State Warriors, as his leadership and 35.2 points average saw Durant named as MVP. He now shows off his superstar jump shot with the Brooklyn Nets.

JOEL EMBIID

THIS GENTLE GIANT IS AN ALL-STAR AND DEFENSIVE BEAST

PROFILE

Position: centre, power forward
National team: Cameroon
Current team: Philadelphia 76ers
Born: 16 March, 1994
Height: 2 m 13 cm
(7 ft)

Born in Cameroon, Joel 'The Process' Embiid made the move from Africa to the NBA to become a pro basketballer, aged 16. After injury delayed his debut with the Philadelphia 76ers, he was finally able to live up to his potential and show off his silky shooting skills, quickly becoming a fan favourite. The three-time NBA All-Star is still only in his mid-20s with his best years ahead of him.

54

Towering shooting guard Harden began his career with the Oklahoma City Thunder, before a surprise switch to the Houston Rockets in 2012, where his pro game reached new heights. Consistently among the candidates for MVP each season, his finest performance was his record 60-point triple-double in January 2018, the first in NBA history. That year he was named NBA MVP, the third player in Rockets' history to earn the honour.

JAMES HARDEN

'THE BEARD' HAS GROWN TO BECOME ONE OF NBA'S ELITE PLAYERS

PROFILE

Position: shooting guard
National team: USA
Current team: Houston Rockets
Born: 26 August, 1989
Height: 1 m 96 cm
(6 ft 5 in)

LEBRON JAMES

THE LAKERS' SUPERSTAR IS A FAN-FAVOURITE

This superstar forward's stats were so impressive that the Cleveland Cavaliers picked him straight from high school. He progressed to become the youngest player ever to score 30,000 points in the NBA, earning him the nickname of King James. Standing tall at 2 m 06 cm, he led the Miami Heat to back-to-back titles in 2012 and 2013 and returned to help Cleveland claim their first title in 2016. He's an Olympic gold medallist with the USA to boot!

Position: point guard
National team: USA
Current team: Oklahoma City
Thunder
Born: 6 May, 1985
Height: 1 m 85 cm
(6 ft 1in)

CHRIS PAUL
A FAST-THINKING PLAYER, HE'S A MASTER OF THE COURT

Paul's speed, vision and solid defence have made him a ten-time All-Star and arguably the top point guard in the NBA. His stats each season for assists and steals are always among the premier players. His rise to stardom began with New Orleans where he made Rookie of the Year in 2006. Paul went on to claim two Olympic gold medals with his national side, USA. Now with his fourth franchise, Oklahoma City Thunder, Paul's dream remains the same – to win his first NBA championship before retirement beckons.

57

PROFILE

Position: small forward
National team: UK
Current team: Le Mans Sarthe
Born: 7 February, 1991
Height: 2 m 01 cm
(6 ft 7 in)

OVIE SOKO

THIS BRITISH LION IS ONE OF EUROPE'S FINEST

58

Small forward Soko is a British baller who lines up for the London Lions. Growing up in the United States, the globe-trotting forward began his pro career in France and has since played in the top leagues in Greece, Italy, Spain and England, establishing himself as one of the best British players in Europe. Soko has also represented the Great Britain national side. Off the court, he has starred in the British TV show *Love Island*.

RUSSELL WESTBROOK
A POPULAR POINT GUARD AND SUPER SLAM-DUNKER

PROFILE

. . . .

Position: point guard
National team: USA
Current team: Houston Rockets
Born: 12 November, 1988
Height: 1 m 91 cm
(6 ft 3 in)

Number 0 for the Houston Rockets, Westbrook has been named an All-Star an incredible nine times over a fine career in basketball. His game combines energy and hard work with stellar scoring, with many points earned from explosive slam dunks. In 2019, he overtook Magic Johnson's triple-doubles figure and is now second in all-time NBA history. On the international stage, Westbrook has won two gold medals with the United States.

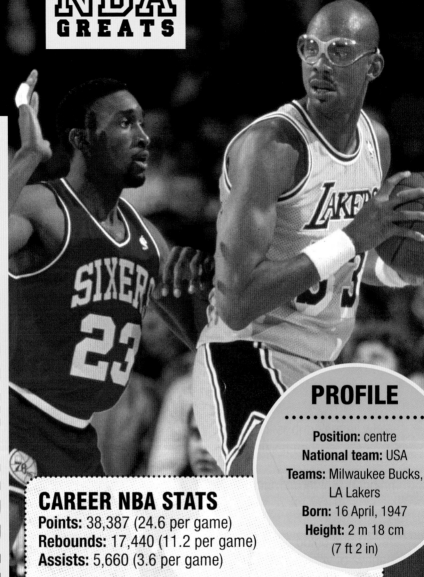

KAREEM ABDUL-JABBAR

A TOWERING TALENT WHO WAS AT THE TOP OF HIS GAME FOR TWO DECADES

PROFILE

Position: centre
National team: USA
Teams: Milwaukee Bucks, LA Lakers
Born: 16 April, 1947
Height: 2 m 18 cm (7 ft 2 in)

CAREER NBA STATS

Points: 38,387 (24.6 per game)
Rebounds: 17,440 (11.2 per game)
Assists: 5,660 (3.6 per game)

Classy centre Kareem Abdul-Jabbar enjoyed incredible success on the court, playing in the NBA for 20 years. Known for his famous 'skyhook' shot, he became the league's all-time top scorers playing for the Milwaukee Bucks and the LA Lakers. By the time he retired in 1989, aged 42, no NBA player had ever scored more points, blocked more shots, won more MVP Awards, played in more All-Star Games or completed more seasons.

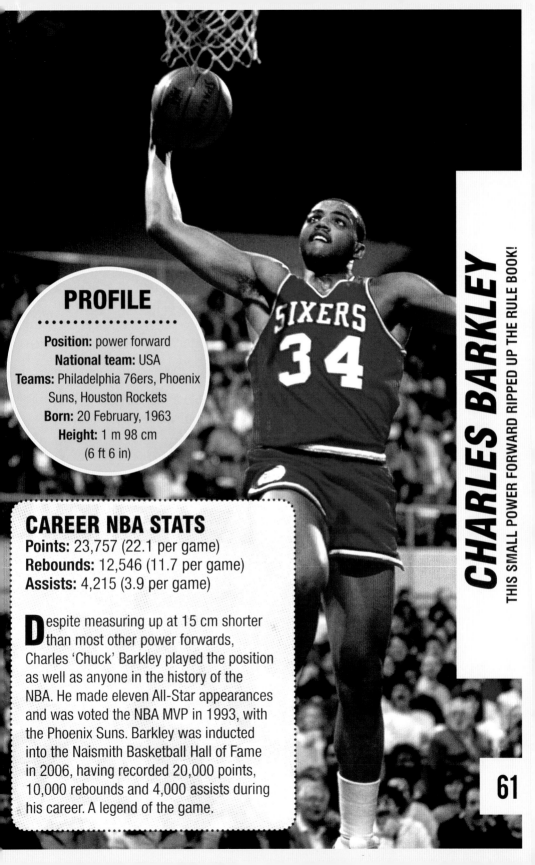

PROFILE

· · · · · · · · · · · · · · · · · · · ·

Position: power forward
National team: USA
Teams: Philadelphia 76ers, Phoenix
Suns, Houston Rockets
Born: 20 February, 1963
Height: 1 m 98 cm
(6 ft 6 in)

CAREER NBA STATS

Points: 23,757 (22.1 per game)
Rebounds: 12,546 (11.7 per game)
Assists: 4,215 (3.9 per game)

Despite measuring up at 15 cm shorter than most other power forwards, Charles 'Chuck' Barkley played the position as well as anyone in the history of the NBA. He made eleven All-Star appearances and was voted the NBA MVP in 1993, with the Phoenix Suns. Barkley was inducted into the Naismith Basketball Hall of Fame in 2006, having recorded 20,000 points, 10,000 rebounds and 4,000 assists during his career. A legend of the game.

CHARLES BARKLEY

THIS SMALL POWER FORWARD RIPPED UP THE RULE BOOK!

LARRY BIRD

PROFILE

Position: small forward, power forward
National team: USA
Teams: Boston Celtics
Born: 7 December, 1956
Height: 2 m 06 cm (6 ft 9 in)

CAREER NBA STATS

Points: 21,791 (24.3 per game)
Rebounds: 8,974 (10.0 per game)
Assists: 5,695 (6.3 per game)

Classy and hardworking, Bird was the pride of the Boston Celtics for thirteen seasons. Fans flocked to see the famous forward! Nicknamed 'Larry the Legend', Bird is also one of just three players in NBA history to win three league MVP awards in a row, claimed in the 1980s. He won a gold medal at the 1992 Barcelona Olympic Games, as part of the USA's 'Dream Team' and went on to work as a top NBA coach and franchise president.

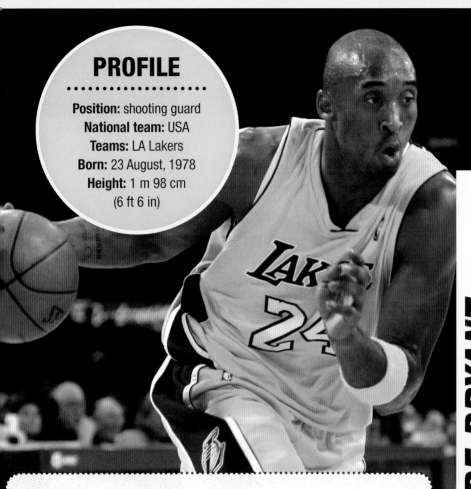

PROFILE

· ·

Position: shooting guard
National team: USA
Teams: LA Lakers
Born: 23 August, 1978
Height: 1 m 98 cm
(6 ft 6 in)

KOBE BRYANT

A FREE-SCORING CENTRE GUARD AND LAKERS' FAN FAVOURITE

CAREER NBA STATS

Points: 33,643 (25.0 per game)
Rebounds: 7,047 (5.2 per game)
Assists: 6,306 (4.7 per game)

Kobe Bryant was an 18-time All-Star who won five NBA championships and became one of the greatest basketball players of his generation, during a 20-year career with the Los Angeles Lakers. The talented centre guard won Olympic gold medals with the brilliant USA team, in 2008 and 2012. Bryant retired in 2016 after scoring 60 points in his final NBA game. He sadly passed away in 2020, following a helicopter accident.

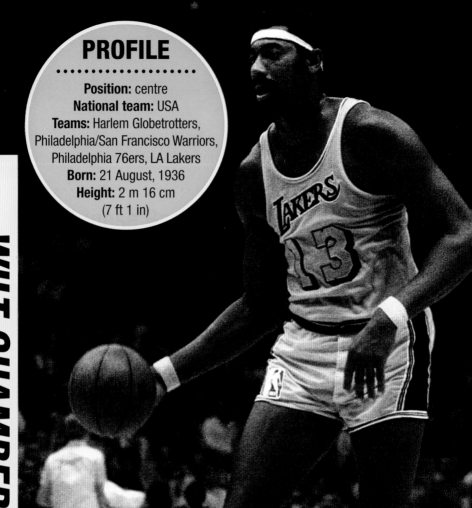

PROFILE

Position: centre
National team: USA
Teams: Harlem Globetrotters,
Philadelphia/San Francisco Warriors,
Philadelphia 76ers, LA Lakers
Born: 21 August, 1936
Height: 2 m 16 cm
(7 ft 1 in)

CAREER NBA STATS

Points: 31,419 (30.1 per game)
Rebounds: 23,924 (22.9 per game)
Assists: 4,643 (4.4 per game)

Standing tall at over seven feet, Chamberlain was an unstoppable NBA centre, who loved to score in the 'paint'. He regularly scored 50 plus points per game with ease and once earned 4,000 points in a single season. His most memorable performance came in 1962, when he scored 100 points for the Philadelphia Warriors against the New York Knicks. He remains the only player in NBA history to reach an incredible century in a single match.

PROFILE

Position: power forward, centre
National team: USA
Teams: San Antonio Spurs
Born: 25 April, 1976
Height: 2 m 11 cm
(6 ft 11 in)

TIM DUNCAN

AN EXPERT BLOCKER AND FIVE-TIME NBA CHAMPION WITH THE SPURS

CAREER NBA STATS

Points: 26,496 (19.0 per game)
Rebounds: 15,091 (10.8 per game)
Assists: 4,225 (3.0 per game)

From the moment he burst on to the scene with the San Antonio Spurs during the 1998 season, rookie Duncan dominated the NBA. He was less flashy than other players on and off the court, but remained one of the game's toughest opponents, playing mostly as a power forward. The Spurs retired his number 21 jersey in 2016 – a fitting tribute to the man who now helps coach the side.

CAREER NBA STATS

Points: 30,026 (24.2 per game)
Rebounds: 10,525 (8.5 per game)
Assists: 5,176 (4.2 per game)

Julius Erving, known as 'Dr J' for his wizardry on the court, was an outstanding player of his generation, helping to advance the game of basketball during the 1970s and 80s. The powerful slam-dunker was an excellent all-round player who scored over 18,364 career points, putting him in the top ten all-time scorers (ABA and NBA combined). His artistry and acrobatics left opponents open-mouthed, while Dr J himself remained a humble athlete.

PROFILE

Position: small forward
National team: USA
Teams: Virginia Squires, New York
Nets, Philadelphia 76ers
Born: 22 February, 1950
Height: 2 m 01 cm
(6 ft 7 in)

Position: point guard
National team: USA
Teams: LA Lakers, Magic M7 Borås (Sweden), Magic Great Danes
Born: 14 August, 1959
Height: 2 m 06 cm
(6 ft 9 in)

MAGIC JOHNSON

A WIZARD ON THE COURT, JOHNSON'S LOVE FOR THE GAME WAS UNMATCHED

CAREER NBA STATS

Points: 17,707 (19.5 per game)
Rebounds: 6,559 (7.2 per game)
Assists: 10,141 (11.2 per game)

Earvin 'Magic' Johnson was a revolutionary player who inspired generations of players to take up basketball. Five championships, three MVP awards and a 12-time All-Star, Johnson did it all over 13 years with the Los Angeles Lakers. As a child he practised all day and even slept with his basketball! A gold medal with the original 'Dream Team' at the 1992 Barcelona Olympics Games was another career highlight for this extraordinary point guard.

MICHAEL JORDAN
BASKETBALL'S G.O.A.T. WAS A SCORING SENSATION!

CAREER NBA STATS
Points: 32,292 (30.1 per game)
Rebounds: 6,672 (6.2 per game)
Assists: 5,633 (5.3 per game)

With his pace, power and mega points-scoring, many consider Michael Jordan to be basketball's greatest player of all time. From the moment he burst on to the scene in 1984, winning Rookie of the Year with the Chicago Bulls, everything he touched turned to gold, as he helped the NBA to go global and win fans around the world. The five-time MVP and six-time NBA champion retired with the league's highest-scoring average of 30.1 points per game in 2003. His 'Air Jordan' range of basketball shoes and sportswear remains an iconic brand.

PROFILE
• • • • • • • • • • • • • • • • • • •
Position: shooting guard, small forward
National team: USA
Teams: Chicago Bulls, Washington Wizards
Born: 17 February, 1963
Height: 1 m 98 cm
(6 ft 6 in)

PROFILE

· · · · · · · · · · · · · · · · · ·

Position: centre
National team: USA
Teams: Orlando Magic, LA Lakers, Miami Heat, Phoenix Suns, Cleveland Cavaliers, Boston Celtics
Born: 6 March, 1972
Height: 2 m 16 cm
(7 ft 1 in)

SHAQUILLE O'NEAL

ONE OF BASKETBALL'S HEAVYWEIGHTS, O'NEAL WAS AN UNSTOPPABLE FORCE

CAREER NBA STATS

Points: 28,596 (23.7 per game)
Rebounds: 13,099 (10.9 per game)
Assists: 3,026 (2.5 per game)

A loved and adored figure, O'Neal's brute power was his greatest asset. At 2 m 16 cm and weighing in at 147 kg (23 st), the centre ate opposition players for breakfast! A former Rookie of the Year and MVP, his slam-dunking technique was legendary. His eight seasons with the LA Lakers saw O'Neal win three championships in a row from 2000 to 2002 and he appeared in the 2004 NBA Finals. He won two gold medals with the USA, at the 1994 FIBA World Cup and 1996 Atlanta Olympic Games.

ULTIMATE FAN QUIZ

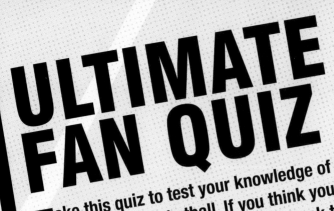

Take this quiz to test your knowledge of the slam-dunking spot that is basketball. If you think you're already a basketball champion, get a friend to ask the questions without sharing the answer options.

1. Who invented the sport of basketball?

- ○ **A.** James Naismith.
- ○ **B.** Street players.
- ○ **C.** Kareem Abdul-Jabbar.

2. What were the first basketball goals made from?

- ○ **A.** Fishing nets.
- ○ **B.** Tin buckets.
- ○ **C.** Peach baskets.

3. What does NBA stand for?

- ○ **A.** National Basketball Alliance.
- ○ **B.** National Basketball Association.
- ○ **C.** Nice Baller Authority.

4. Which position is usually played by the smallest players?

- ○ **A.** Centre.
- ○ **B.** Point guard.
- ○ **C.** Power forward.

5. Basketball is an Olympic sport.
○ **A.** True.
○ **B.** False.

6. Which NBA side changed its name from the Pelicans to the Hornets?
○ **A.** Chicago.
○ **B.** San Antonio.
○ **C.** New Orleans.

7. Who was the youngest player to reach 30,000 points in the NBA?
○ **A.** LeBron James.
○ **B.** Stephen Curry.
○ **C.** Wilt Chamberlain.

8. How many times did Kobe Bryant win the NBA championship?
○ **A.** Once.
○ **B.** Four.
○ **C.** Five.

9. How many points are awarded for a shot in the paint?
○ **A.** One.
○ **B.** Two.
○ **C.** Three.

10. What is the nickname of the London-based BBL club?

○ **A.** Raiders.
○ **B.** Scorchers.
○ **C.** Lions.

The ref's whistle blows! Check your answers below and add up how many questions you got right to reveal your score.

1. A – James Naismith; **2. C** – Peach baskets; **3. B** – National Basketball Association; **4. B** – Point guard; **5. A** – True; **6. C** – New Orleans; **7. A** LeBron James; **8. C** – Five; **9. B** – Two; **10. C** – Lions.

0–3 correct answers
FAIRWEATHER FAN!
Some extra training is needed to become a basketball fanatic.

4–7 correct answers
SUPER FAN!
You shoot, you score! A strong performance!

8–10 correct answers
CHAMPION FAN!
You slam-dunked this quiz – you're a basketball pro!

Show your true colours! Design a slick new kit for your team below.

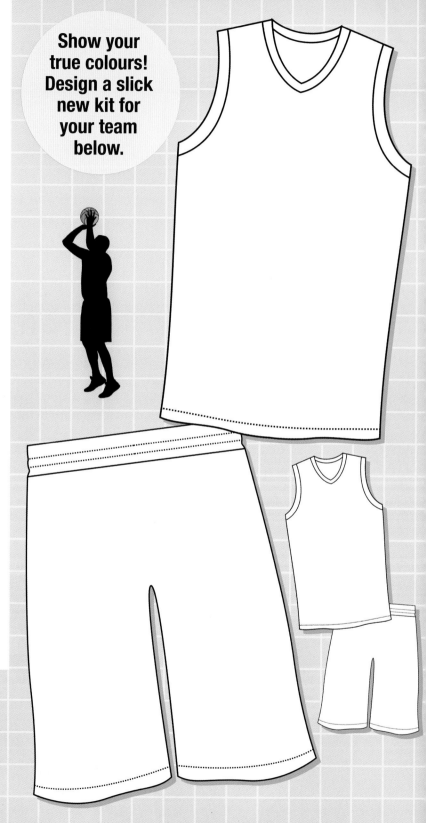

Now create a shoe design to help you tear up the court.

AIRBALL
A shot at the basket that misses everything – including the rim, backboard and net.

ALL-STAR
An outstanding player. An All-Star team or game is made up of top pro players.

ASSIST
A pass that comes immediately before – and sets up – a scored basket.

BACKBOARD
The rectangular piece of wood or fibreglass to which the rim is attached.

BANK SHOT
A shot that bounces off the backboard and into the hoop.

BENCH
The substitute basketball players.

BLOCKING
When a defender uses their body to illegally prevent an opponent from passing them.

CARRYING
When a player briefly holds the ball from underneath, carrying it while dribbling, resulting in a foul.

CHEST PASS
A two-handed pass thrown from a player's chest in a straight line to the chest area of the receiver.

DEFENCE
The act of preventing the offence from scoring or the basketball team without the ball.

FIELD GOAL
A basket scored on any shot other than a free throw, worth two or three points, depending on the distance from the basket.

G.O.A.T
Used to mean 'greatest of all time'.

IN THE PAINT
The 'paint' is the area inside the lane lines from the baseline to the free-throw line. Two points are awarded when a player shoots the ball through the hoop from anywhere inside the three-point line. If an offensive player has a foot on or inside these lines for three seconds or longer, they will be called for the three-second violation. There is no restriction on the time defensive players can occupy the paint.

JUMP BALL
When an official tosses the ball into play, then two opposing players jump to win possession of the ball.

JUMP SHOT
A shot that is released after the shooter has jumped into the air.

LAY-UP
A close-up shot taken after dribbling to the basket.

MVP
Short for **'Most Valuable Player'** – the player who has performed the best in a match or series.

OFFENCE
The attacking team, with possession of the ball.

OVERTIME
An extra period played at the end of a game, if the scores are tied.

PIVOT
When a player keeps one foot on the court while moving the other to make a pass or shot.

REBOUND
When a player gains control of the ball following a missed shot that has bounced off the rim or backboard.

ROOKIE OF THE YEAR
A Rookie of the Year award is given by a number of sports leagues to the top-performing athlete in his or her first season within the league.

SIDELINES
The two boundary lines that run the length of the court.

SLAM DUNK
When a player scores by forcefully placing the ball through the basket from above.

TIMEOUT
When play is temporarily suspended by an official, or at the request of a team to treat an injured player or discuss tactics.

TRAVELLING
When the player handling the ball takes too many steps without dribbling, resulting in a foul. Also known as walking.

TURNOVER
When the offensive team loses possession due to committing a foul, steal or out-of-bounds violation.

INDEX

PICTURE CREDITS

While every effort has been made to credit all contributors, we would like to apologize should there be any omissions or errors, and would be pleased to make any appropriate corrections for future editions of this book.

Front cover (from left to right): Mitchell Layton/Gettyimages; Jesse D. Garrabrant/Gettyimages; Alex Livesey/Stringer/Gettyimages; Jerry Wachter/Gettyimages; Fred Lee/Getty images.
Back cover (from left to right): Alex Livesey/Stringer/Gettyimages; Jerry Wachter/Gettyimages.

Internal images (from left to right):

P5, P8, P30–31, P42, P58, P70 Alex Livesey/Stringer/Gettyimages; P5, P13, P23, P32–33, P38, P52, P56, P70, P73, P76 Jesse D. Garrabrant/Gettyimages; P5, P8, P15, P18, P30, P38, P68, P70, P73 P77, Jerry Wachter/Gettyimages; P5, P8, P47, P70 Mitchell Layton/ Gettyimages; P5, P26, P35, P40, P70, P77 Fred Lee/Getty images; P27, P64 Wen Roberts/Gettyimages; P27, P67 Richard Mackson/ Gettyimages; P31, P54 Chris Schwegler/Gettyimages; P61, P69 Andrew D. Bernstein/Gettyimages; P37, P62 Nathaniel S. Butler/ Gettyimages; P28, P65 Chris Birck/Gettyimages; P50 Jonathan Daniel/Gettyimages; P66 Jim Cummins/Gettyimages; P51, P72 Jonathan Ferrey/Gettyimages; P55 Ronald Martinez/Gettyimages; P29, P57 Omar Rawlings/Gettyimages; P59 Tim Warner/ Gettyimages; P35, P39, P60, P71 Mike Powell/Gettyimages; P53 Al Belo/Gettyimages; P7, P63, P71, P72 Stephen Dunn/Gettyimages; P48 Moto Yoshimura/Gettyimages.